My Life Through Mirror Glasses

Teenell White

This book is dedicated to those dealing with Multiple Sclerosis that are trying to find their way. It is also dedicated to people that want more out of life that come from nothing or less than nothing.

My name is Teenell White. I was born May 15th, 1979 and raised in Kinston, North Carolina. I am married to a wonderful husband of 17 great years, Pierre White. My two boys Jalill, 21 and Emerald, 11. My father Gerry Branch, a factory worker, was deceased at age 45 due to congestive heart failure. That was one of the hardest days of my life receiving a phone call to head to the hospital. When I arrived, he was already pronounced dead. Looking at him lifeless on the stretcher, I just couldn't believe it. I had talked with him the night before. He was telling me how much he loved me and if I needed anything I could call him. Now, all of a sudden, I could never call or hear his voice again. My entire body grew numb. My mind was clouded, and I had no words. My father was gone forever.

When I was 18 years old, I didn't realize how young my father was. He was such a hard worker, but he had so many health problems. He had always been a heavyset and overweight man. However, before he died, he was trying to get his weight under control. He even purchased a treadmill to start his journey. I was so proud that he made that decision to start exercising. Slow progress was so much better than no progress. My father was an army veteran. So, I knew he could get his weight under control. This was a must because he was diagnosed with congestive heart failure, high blood pressure, high cholesterol. He had a list of health problems as well as a list of meds to take on a daily basis. Also, he had an enlarged heart. The doctors suggested a heart transplant, but my dad was not on broad for that type of surgery. The doctors told him his life expectancy was short without one. I didn't know how to feel about that. On the one hand, I wanted him to have surgery. However, on the other hand, I didn't want anything to happen during the surgery and him not pull through. Therefore, I respected his decision not to have surgery.

My father was my hero and Superman. I felt things would be fine. He taught me morals, respect and made sure I had men in my life that were going to treat me right. That man had to treat me like a princess and put me totally first. Anyone that wanted to date me or take me out had to go through my dad for approval. My husband now made the cut. I never had a man that wanted to get to know all of me, as well as my flaws and accept me for me who I was. He was crazy in love with me, and I was crazy in love with him. I felt at peace that my dad was ok and pleased with my choice of my guy. I am not saying he didn't give my husband a hard time, but he earned my dad's respect.

My dad also tried to instill in our family the importance of having your own business. My dad was not a fan of working for someone. Even though he did what he had to do for our family, he really wanted to work for himself. He was always at the flea markets in North Carolina selling goods. I admired him so much. He never missed work. Never. I wanted to exceed his expectations and make him so proud of me. One day I accomplished and did just that!

My mom, Nancy Branch, a living widow retired factory worker. She quit her factory job to stay home and take care of my dad. She never complained, and she stepped up to the plate and did what a wife supposed to do. She took care of him until his death. She was so strong through it all. I'm not sure if my strength would have been like my mom's. She kept it together through the funeral and all. I'm not sure if I could have done any of it. I would have wanted to die myself. My mother's love, dedication, and commitment to my dad and their marriage was God's love. Throughout all the years of my dad's passing, she still held it together. I knew she missed him dearly. Her faith was first and foremost in our family. We went to Sunday School and church every Sunday. If you didn't, you weren't allowed to go outside to play. She never drunk alcohol, smoke cigarettes, and was everything that a true Christian should be. I wanted to be like her as a wife. She took care of her children and kept food on the table for us. I was raised in a two-parent home. I am not saying everything and every day was great, but my parents took me, my brother and sister on family trips every summer. They even invited some of our cousins to come along to Kings Dominion, Beach Trips, Bush Gardens, and Carowinds. They made sure we had fun and that we were a family. Being raised in the south, you get accustomed to good food. In other words, unhealthy foods. Lots of fried country soul fool. When there isn't anyone to teach you nutrition because my parents weren't taught nutrition.... whose fault is it? The cycle has got to be broken. We have to teach our children the importance of a balanced meal. For my family, my parents had to feed three children. I have two older siblings one brother Gary Branch and a sister Tracy Branch both living and doing well. My siblings both went through their trials and areas in life, but I continued to pray for them both and my entire family.

Being the baby, the last child wasn't easy. I didn't want extra attention nor did I want to feel as though my parents gave me everything. I can honestly say with being the baby at the time, it wouldn't have been that horrible to get an extra treat. My siblings did feel some type of way. Yes, it put stress on our relationship as siblings. That issue was never resolved. Sometimes the subject is still brought up from previous years before. Forgiveness in the heart has to be sought out, and we have to go back to putting God first. I never knew small things in life were major issues for some later on in life. There are small holes that bandages can't fix. Only God can fill those small holes.

For years no one was really honest about it or told me how they truly felt. What I learned from that experience was to make sure I treated my kids equal no matter what. I never wanted one of my kids to feel less loved, less appreciated, less wanted or cared for. My parents were not perfect, to say the least. I can honestly say they did the best they could with what they had. For two people to stay together and make things work, through heartache, pain, and sickness, I felt that God's love was in the midst of things. That's what kept my parents together until my father passed. We never went hungry, that's a fact. With trying to keep food on the table and bills paid nutrition was nonexistent. Keeping the bills paid and full stomachs were a priority. My parents did the best they could with what they had. School was very important in my family. My school days were ok. Nothing special. I did enjoy receiving certificates for the A&B honor roll. At times, I was the underdog. Most didn't care too much for me. I was basically overlooked, and friends were seasonal.

Most people's intentions as far as starting a friendship with me, I was unsure of. I never tried to judge because I always gave everyone a fair shot in my life. Everyone deserves an open door to trust. Trust is a hard thing to have and an even harder thing to keep. Once trust is broken it's always hard to regain or build again. You're never able to trust anyone fully once the trust is broken. It's like it never existed. What I have learned about friendships is that true friendships will be there for you no matter what. That's why my husband has always been my best friend. There have been times when I didn't understand the true meaning of a best friend because my perspective was all wrong. I was so off and in left field because sisterhood is how I labeled a best friend. I found out quickly that wasn't the case. A best friend for me is not a title placed upon someone but something that is earned and wanted. Something known, but not forced to be. In this life, I didn't ever want anyone in that position again as a best friend. My husband has that spot, period. He has it for life. Associates yes, friends yes, best friend no. That's friendship in a nutshell. I always felt people looked at me as though they were doing me a favor to be my friend, but in actuality, I was doing them a favor. I never sought out to be mean or hurt anyone, but people brought that to me.   I didn't understand why, but my husband tells me now, that I was pretty and most were jealous. It's crazy how people need favors now when they were the one trying to fight or bully me after school. I never forget anything or a face. I have forgiven most but haven't forgotten. My brother and sister...we had each other backs. Couldn't mess with one without dealing with all of us. My grades were decent because my father didn't play when it came to making bad grades. When I first started grade school I struggled. I remember the 3rd grade and having to have a tutor because I just wasn't interested or focused. However, I Thank God for this one lady teacher because she really helped me and used her time after school at her house to tutor me. It's crazy because both my boys struggle the same way. One teacher told my youngest that he could get a job using his hands, like college wasn't an option for him. I told her he would succeed and he will go to college.

Being born prematurely, my youngest had a rough start. Everything started late for him, even his speech. He just pointed to everything and never said a word. Me and my husband were concerned. He constantly stayed sick because he was in daycare. Ear infections after infection and at 14 months old he still struggled to talk. We finally took him to see an ear, nose and throat doctor. The decision was made to put tub placements in his ears. My husband and I were so scared. Our baby boy's first surgery. We both held our emotions inside. We held it together so our baby wouldn't be afraid. After the surgery, our son talked immediately. It's crazy that the entire time our son was having a hearing problem and that's why he couldn't talk. All of this time...God is just so good. I never counted him out as far as a learning disability. My son is a very special child in every way. No one will label my two boys or put them in a box. They both will do extraordinary things. I can't wait for the chapters of their lives to be writing. My oldest was the first to go to a four-year college. He doesn't really understand how proud I am of him.

I brag about him every day. Words cannot even begin to express my feeling about his success.

My school days were very important to my parents especially my dad. Every report card, if you made bad grades, you were on punishment until the next report card came out. I really appreciate that now because getting a college education is so important and it starts at home. I stress that to both my boys. My oldest is in college, and my youngest will succeed and go to college as well. High School was not good for me. I was totally over school and didn't care too much for it. 9th grade was cool because my brother and sister were seniors and everyone got to meet their baby sister. So, my grades weren't a priority anymore. I was trying to figure out who I was and not sure what I wanted to do with my life. My parent's income wasn't much, and my grades sucked, so a 4year college was out of the question or so I thought.

My dream was to go to school and get an education, but my parents couldn't afford it. My 12th-grade year I got pregnant with my first son. I was unable to graduate with my class in 1997 because I was nine months pregnant and about to give birth. I received my diploma at the community college that fall semester. My firstborn made me grow up and look at life differently. He made me want to strive for success because I wanted to provide a better life for him. I had to provide and be a good mom. So, that's what I set out to do. At a very young age, I always wanted genuine love....to give and receive that back. God sent my wonderful husband at the age of 18 years old. God has just been with me my entire life, protecting me, loving me, when I truly didn't deserve it. I made a lot of stupid mistakes. Being so young, finances, saving money, and paying bills on time was not a priority. Surviving was a priority. Just making it and making rent was important. I was going to school full time and working part-time. I told myself at least I had to have my associate degree and that's what I did in applied science in Medical Assistant.

Things were looking up, but I still was not satisfied. I had a full-time job at a doctor's office, my significant other worked full time. Things were ok. We decided to get married in December 2001. One of the happiest days of my life. I had a man that loved me unconditional. It was a God sent, and heaven-sent kind of love because our story just picked up where it left off. I met him in physical science in 9th grade. We both liked each other, but the timing wasn't right. Things always happen for a reason and in God's time. We were so young when we got together, basically babies. So, we had to find out who we were individually and together. One thing we knew we had was unconditional love for each other, and that was never going to change. Something in my spirit was telling me I deserved more and I needed more. My oldest was the only child at the time. I felt as though we needed another addition to the family. So, my husband and I decided 10 years later to have my youngest son. He is nothing but love, and my youngest is a mirror reflection. My fight is for my children, and my willingness to never stop trying to achieve my goals are for them.

Then I really started thinking about my life. What about a house, what about saving money, what about my credit? I guess all in due time, in God's time. My husband and I weren't ready for the responsibility. Forwarding my life to 2010 where my life took a twist. I started my fitness journey. I wanted to get healthy and exercise because after having my boys I just didn't make it a priority at all. I wasn't comfortable in my own skin. Even though I wore my figure well, I didn't like the image looking back at me. I wanted to go to a clothing store and not be limited to what I could wear because of my size. Or feel ashamed because I let my weight and health get out of control. I can admit that I did just that. I gave up totally. In high school, I was a small size, but no one would have known because I dressed in baggy clothes. Knocking on about 190lbs close to 200lbs and in size 16-18 jeans after having my children, I knew that I had to grab hold of my life. So, my first step was walking. I walked with friends after work until dark sometimes. Lost my first 20lbs just walking.

I was so determined to get the weight off, and I lost a total of 60lbs. Through walking and Zumba fitness I was able to maintain and keep it off. Zumba Fitness gave me life. To be able to dance, have fun and burn calories at the same time, I was sold. They say when you lose weight things start to surface. I'm a true believer of that now. I got my license to teach Zumba fitness in June 2012 when all the craziness of being sick with no answers started in 2011. Nothing and I mean nothing was going to stop what God had planned for me. I wanted to be a leader and change lives. I wanted to use my gift from God, and my plan was to do just that.

No one in my entire family has been diagnosed with an autoimmune disease. I guess I was the chosen one. How I initially found out was because I was very sick starting in May 2011. I had numbness and tingling from my abdomen all the way down to both right and left legs to both feet. My ability to walk normally was fading away right before my eyes. I didn't want to believe that my chances of my husband taking care of me in a wheelchair was very high. I could feel the nerve impulses throughout my body as though something was happening and I could only tell my husband because everyone else would think I was crazy. And I was right because the doctors thought I was actually crazy. I honestly couldn't believe it. I was living in a real-life nightmare. I was released from the hospital the day before my birthday on May 14th, 2011 and referred to a neurologist to see if they could solve and get some answers on what was happening. He thought it was possibly symptoms of a common cold. I was looked at crazy. I felt uncomfortable at times because what I was going through sounded insane. How could I explain my symptoms while none of it made sense to me? Therefore, I knew that it wouldn't make sense to the doctor. I thought he would think I was probably insane. I had no control over what was going on inside of my body. Basically, I have to live with whatever was going inside forever. Labwork was taken on that visit to the doctor. Then I was sent on my way. I felt like a number. I wasn't important at all. My symptoms and problems meant nothing. I walked out the same way I came in, with no answer. Still living and feeling like I was in a real-life nightmare. I felt as though I was on an assembly line and I was getting passed along to whoever wanted to hear my story or problems. Take a number, and we will get back with you.

Thankfully a follow-up appointment made because my symptoms were no better and I was one sick person. Lab work was positive for possible multiple sclerosis. So, the next thing to do was to perform an LP- lumbar puncture, which was scheduled for the next visit. The procedure of taking fluid from the spine in the lower back through a hollow needle. Oh my Gosh! After having that procedure done, I couldn't even hold my head up the next day because of an excruciating headache. I was at work..... mind you. No one told me I needed to lay flat after the procedure for the next couple, of days and I also had to get pain medication through an IV to help with the pain.

I still continued to push through and work my job. As I said before my God continued to be with me through it all. Next up I had to get an MRI of my brain and spine. The results came back from the Lumbar puncture positive and MRI positive for lesions of my brain and spine confirming the diagnosis of Multiple Sclerosis in August 2011. Now the doctor was finally taking me somewhat seriously. One thing I wasn't going to do was allow someone to make life-changing decisions on my life without me having any say so. With that being said I made the final decision whether the doctor agreed or not. It's my body, my life. So many people allow others to make decisions about their healthcare. I never believed in taking alot of medication for anything. My faith and my God are my medications. At the doctor's office the day of the initial news I didn't cry, but I was more confused and not understanding about why this disease has been put upon me. Multiple Sclerosis is a chronic autoimmune disease typically a progressive disease involving damage to the myelin sheaths of nerve cells in the brain and spinal cord, whose symptoms may include numbness, impairment of speech and of the muscular coordination, blurred vision and also really severe fatigue. I remembered that God puts nothing on us that we can't bear. So, I never claimed it. You say I have this disease, but my God says I don't. I'm healed in the name of Jesus. I told myself that I would do what was necessary to stay alive.

We discussed treatment options, and I decided to go with a newly pill form medication. I was on it for 6 months taken by mouth once daily which wasn't hard at all. Then an MRI was scheduled for 6 months to see if the medication was slowing the progression down. MRI results said no. Ok, another roadblock. Walking was getting better, numbness and tingling getting better but results are even worse. Ok another treatment option, pill form medication taken by mouth daily. On it for 5yrs no flare-ups......each MRI showed little progression. Thankfully, I was able to get my group (AFAA) Aerobic and Fitness Association of America exercise group fitness certification in May of 2015. Nothing was going to stop God's plan. I was feeling good and living my best life. The doctors were stating I was a walking miracle.

Everything was going so well. My husband and I started our 5-year plan. It consisted of our oldest going to college, getting our credit better, buying a home, saving more money and opening my fitness studio. Everything on that list came to pass with hard work and God's favor. There were a lot of no's, a lot of slammed doors, a lot your crazy looks, but God's favor and grace got us through. Six years of wanting to make a difference and change lives through having my very own fitness studio. I was very thankful to be able to share my gifts teaching group fitness at gyms which I was a major impact. The people I met and the lives I changed was amazing, but I wanted my own fitness center. God sent the right people in my path. His grace and favor blew my mind away. I couldn't believe that everything I prayed for, everything I ask for came to life. God showed me his power and made me understand it. I will always will give him the praise and tell everyone it was God and not me that worked this miracle. I did nothing on my own. Through him and only him. All you have to do is trust and believe. I put my work in and was obedient to God. I set out to do something every day to open my fitness studio. I will forever be grateful for the people that gave me a chance and made my vision come to life. I'm even thankful for the slammed doors because that made me work even harder. The maybes and never gave me chance. The "no call backs" because I wasn't important enough. God forced people to see me and his gift. His power was incredible. He granted me with everything I ever asked for. Fast forwarding to 2018. It was after Thanksgiving, and I had not had a flare excerebration in over 4yrs with MS. I never let my diagnosis of multiples sclerosis run my life. Even though the doctors stated that I would have multiple sclerosis for the rest of my life, I never felt sad, depressed, or angry, because once I decided to feel that way, I knew that I would be giving up and letting this disease win. More twists in my life continued to happen. New symptoms started, new ones that I hadn't had before. Even worse this time. I hated calling my neurologist because I was treated like a number again. After calling the neurologist, it took days for a return phone call or no call back at all. Sometimes it would take days for a return phone call. Or after leaving a return phone call message, I still received no call back. When I got so fed up of not hearing back from anyone, I decided to make another phone call. Most of the time the answer would be that no call back was given because the message wasn't received. I thought to myself what is really happening? No one, not even my caregiver cares. That's how I felt. What was going on with me was clearly not important. I was a patient that called when there was a problem going on. Not because I just had extra time on my hands to call and complain. At that moment I realized that I needed to rely on God and no one else. My appointments were always canceled or rescheduled. With everything I was going through, no call back or anything. I prayed to God to get me through, and he did. They call it the (MS) Multiple Sclerosis HUG. The MS hug is a Multiple Sclerosis symptom that feels like there is a tight band around your chest or torso. For me, it felt as though the band was around my abdomen area. If I digested anything, the band would get tighter. It definitely was the worst pain I have ever felt in my life. Imagine someone squeezing the life completely out of you, that's what I felt like. I have had numbness and tingling before but never in my hands. That part was the worse, of the worse. It started in my left thumb and progressed to the entire hand. Then the progression went to my entire right hand. Unable to hold anything or write, pretty much do anything dealing with my hands. Mind you my job is a phlebotomist. I had to take time from work and get intravenously steroid infusion for 5 days due to the severe inflammation. I prayed to God, cried out to God and at this point, I wanted to be on the other side with God because I didn't want to suffer anymore. I cried every day and begged my family to pray for me every day. I honestly thought I wasn't going to make it. The pain was unbearable, the numbness was unreal. I really started thinking about my dad and how I was going to be able to see him real soon. I hated the fact that my thoughts went that far. At that point seeing him didn't seem bad at all. I knew he was in heaven and that is where I would be going, so the thought was beginning to make sense. I actually thought about my husband. He prayed for me and prayed with me every day and night. He even wished the pain upon himself, so I could feel better. He held me in his arms, looked into my eyes and wiped my tears away. He told me to keep fighting because all of this greatness happens for you, so you know the devil has to come in and try to destroy God's plan. I cried every day, every night, on my lunch break. It was crazy what I was going through. The day before my soft opening of my fitness studio December 20, 2018, I was so sick. I had fatigue, could barely move around, I was so weak to walk, numbness and tingling throughout my body, my stomach was tight as bricks, and I had absolutely no appetite. I was contemplating on canceling because I could barely get around. I said to myself if I have to crawl and teach then that's what I will do. I went home and got into God's word and listened to his word all night. I also prayed all night and claimed healing in the name of Jesus.

The next morning, I was doing so much better but my challenges to stay strong is on a daily basis. I have to keep God in me all day. Because to fight the battle of MS is never done. I had to learn that the hard way. Never get comfortable. Stay in God's presence and his word at all times.

I went to church and got this beautiful lady to pray with me about what was going on asking for healing, crying out to God. I claimed it that day sincerely. Not paying attention to what was going on internally but keeping my mind on what God said he had already done. I told him if he got me out of this mess, I will totally commit to him and tell my story. I never will ever take for granted the basic things in life that God allows us to do every day on a daily basis. Wakeup first and foremost, walk, talk, see, feel and the ability to hear. So many people take life for granted. The movements of our body, God's doing. Nothing in this life is guaranteed. It's not a guarantee that you're going to rise out of bed the next day. It's a possibility that your life may be turned upside down. Or you have been diagnosed with Multiple Sclerosis like me and so many people in this world. I thank God for the ability to still be able to walk. Multiple Sclerosis is a disabling disease. There are so many people living with this disease that wish they can move around and not feel pain anymore. I will continue to be that vessel for people like me to walk and continue to move. I pray that God will keep us and that his grace and favor will continue to be upon us. I will continue to move. My journey, my life, God's gift, and my new beginnings started on January 7th, 2019 with the Grand opening and ribbon cutting of Tees Cardio Fitness Center. It was a 6-year dream, and it came to life!

This is God plan! FAITH, GRACE, FAVOR, AND GOD'S LOVE.

www.ingramcontent.com/pod-product-compliance
Lightning Source LLC
Chambersburg PA
CBHW061106050726
47592CB00004B/1847